THOUGHT CATALOG BOOKS

I'm Just Here for the Free Scrutiny

I'm Just Here for the Free Scrutiny

One Model's Tale of Insanity and Inanity in the Wonderful World of Fashion

ABBY ROSMARIN

THOUGHT CATALOG BOOKS

Brooklyn, NY

THOUGHT CATALOG BOOKS

Copyright © 2014 by Abby Rosmarin

All rights reserved. Published by Thought Catalog Books, a division of The Thought & Expression Co., Williamsburg, Brooklyn. Founded in 2010, Thought Catalog is a website and imprint dedicated to your ideas and stories. We publish fiction and non-fiction from emerging and established writers across all genres. For general information and submissions: manuscripts@thoughtcatalog.com.

First print edition, 2016

ISBN 978-1945796166

10 9 8 7 6 5 4 3 2 1

Cover photography by © Abby Rosmarin

Contents

1

Everyone's a Casting Director

"You should model."

When you've been in the 99th percentile in height since you the day were born, it's only a matter of time until someone advises you to model. They'll also advise you to try out for the local basketball team. And to reach that thing on the top shelf for them. It's all just part and parcel of being a tall female.

I didn't start modeling until I was almost 20. Given that a model's "prime" is now as painfully young as 16, I recognized that I was starting out when most models tend to retire. I also recognized that I would be modeling in Boston, which is not exactly a fashion mecca. Or even a fashion holy site. Truth be told, it's barely a fashion place of worship. Recognizing all this, I knew there would be no superstardom in my future.

But I was okay with that. In a way, the best thing I ever did was ignore everyone's advice and wait until I was toeing into my sophomore year of college before I started. The modeling business is rough. You need a strong resolve and an ability to stand your ground. Granted, I barely had that at 20, but I definitely had none of that at 16. If how I had handled my high school relationships were of any indication, I could've enjoyed a lucrative career where people took full advantage of me while I wept quietly and blamed myself and wrote passionately in my diary.

But then again, if that had been the case, this collection of essays probably would have been a lot more entertaining.

Regardless, I ignored what people told me until I decide—independently—to give the whole "modeling" thing a try. I didn't let what people would say sway me because I understood that, at the end of the day, a layperson's advice isn't worth the calories burned to say the words in the first place.

One of the first things you learn as a model is to never—ever—start off any conversation about modeling with, "Everyone said I should model!" Aside from the fact that it is horribly off-putting, it is terribly misguided. At the end of the day, neither your neighbor, nor your boyfriend, nor your auntie is an agency director. They are not fashion photographers. They are not designers looking for the right look to go with their new style.

Most likely.

It would be like if I went up to Buckingham Palace and declared that they needed to accept me as one of their own because, "Daddy always said I was a princess!"

It just makes no damn sense.

Throughout the years, I've learned that the, "You should ›del!" phrase has a thousand various subtexts, ranging from the innocent to the downright predatory. When a family member tells you that you should model, they really just mean that they think you are beautiful (at least beautiful in their eyes). When a guy at the bar tells you that you should model, he really is just saying that he'd enjoy sleeping with you (and is hoping that calling you a model will make you more agreeable). When a dude with a secondhand DSLR camera (that is always set to "Auto") and a studio that is comprised of a wrinkled sheet duct-taped to his living room wall tells you that you should model, he really is just hoping you'll model for him—preferably naked.

These are the thoughts that go through an actual director's mind when they hear some would-be starlet with a glittered crop top and false lashes talk about her modeling aspirations.

So, keeping that bit of information to myself, I started off my career as a freelancer—a base model for a graphic design student here, a model for the cover of a local band's demo track there—before I tried submitting my pictures to agencies. I signed with one Boston agency, which I stayed with until after I graduated college. I eventually began working full-time, and the modeling world became a hobby world for me. If I couldn't do it on nights and weekends, then it just couldn't be done.

Four years later, I quit the real world, with absolutely, positively, no clue where I was going in my life. I decided to do the one thing I couldn't do as a real world "adult": model. I signed with a new agency in Boston and started up my modeling life again, this time as a grown-up commercial model (which is what I call it, since "adult model" has a pretty damning connotation to it).

I can't help but look back on my previous experiences as a model with equal parts amusement and embarrassment. Some experiences were good. Some were not so good. Some were hilarious, while others were the type that you just have to laugh at, lest you go insane. The wonderful world of commercial and fashion modeling is definitely a lot different than what they tell you in the brochure. But, somehow, through trial and error (mostly error), I found my footing. And, despite it all, I will continue to see what little part of the modeling world I can carve out for myself. I'll use my past as a way to bolster me into the future.

Just as soon as I get that thing on the top shelf for that guy.

2
That Thing With Your Face

Okay, someone has to be honest.

You know that thing you do? With your face? With your head and your lips and your cheeks?

Your go-to, "people will think I'm cute in this photo!" face?

Yeah. It's not a good look.

How do I know? Because I did that thing. With my face. With my head and my lips and my cheeks. My go-to, "people will think I'm cute in this photo!" face.

And it's not a good look.

The hardest part for a model who begins her career as a free-lancer is that you don't have anyone around to boldly tell you when you're not doing something right. I worked with a lot of newbie photographers—as well as a lot of experienced photographers who specialized in working with newbie models—when attempting to build my portfolio. The newbie photographer would be too worried that they might be screwing something up to tell me to stop channeling Zoolander. The photographer who specialized in working with newbies would be too busy showering me with unearned praise to tell me when to loosen up and stop looking at the camera like it's going to attack me.

I attempted everything I saw on TV. I sucked in my cheeks. I smiled with my eyes ("smized"!). I tilted my head so much to the side that Paris Hilton circa 2004 would've blushed. I pressed my palms into my stomach in my best "broken doll" pose (or, for us laypeople, the "I have gas!" pose). I smirked and lowered my eyes and gazed pensively out of shot—sometimes all at the same time. I shoved my shoulders forward and angled my hips and did all the things I just knew would make me irresistible.

Only one problem: I could very much resist the girl in the picture. In fact, the only thing I found irresistible was the temptation to call 911, because obviously that model was having a stroke.

But you just don't realize how bad you look at first. I would get the photos back, ooh and aah over the fact that, there I was, in professional picture form, with makeup and everything, and go on with my life. I ignored the tensed shoulders and forced poses and gleefully saved every single picture to my hard drive.

However, like Prince Charming's kiss for Aurora, all it took was one photographer's comment to break the spell.

"You look like you're on the verge of crying."

I was about four or five "portfolio building" photo shoots in when I heard a photographer say that. And, exactly as if some-one had woken me from a deep slumber, I saw my pictures in a brand new way.

Suddenly, all I could see was how ridiculous I looked. Sucking in my cheeks didn't emphasize my cheekbones; it gave me duck face. The "broken doll" pose didn't add an element of high fashion to the shoot; it added a level of ridiculousness as I posed in casual wear in front of some abandoned railroad tracks (and you haven't truly modeled until you've done the trite "pose by some railroad tracks" shoot). My back was oddly hunched and my shoulders were practically by my ears. My "come hither" look was about as convincing as an 8-year-old pageant girl's stare.

To be frank, I looked silly.

It took a long while before I finally found my groove. Some photographers would gently direct me out of crappy poses. Others would shower me with flattery, even as I started resort-ing back to Duck Face. Others deliberately directed me into said crappy postures, as if I were a middle-aged housewife who had hired them to take clichéd boudoir pictures of me for my husband. I studied other models, attempted to copy what they did, and tried to figure out where I going astray.

I repeated this process over and over and over again until I realized something very important: while I was busy think-ing about what does and doesn't work, I didn't realize that I was simply thinking too much. I was posing for the camera while every single fiber of my being was screaming, "This is what I'm supposed to do, right? This makes the pictures nice, right?"

And it showed. It all looked artificial and forced.

To date, my most successful photo shoots—and my most lucrative jobs—always came as a result of me going in without thinking too much. This doesn't exactly help curtail the "models are mindless" belief, but the best photos came when I simply just…moved. I stopped thinking and worrying so much and did whatever felt right. The second I thought about it was the second I tensed up, got awkward, and looked into the camera like I was an international kidnapping victim creating a video to air on CNN.

"Dear America: I am fine. I am being treated well. Please do what the captors want. The well-groomed, oddly-fashionable captors."

In some cruel twist of fate, I'm still trying not to think too much in regular, real life snapshots. I'll smile by tourist attractions like said hostage, trying to prove that my benevolent abductors take me site-seeing. I'll awkwardly bend one knee like I'm trying to sell stockings in an impromptu family photo. So that thing I do, with my face, and my cheeks, is still there in real life. And it's going to take some time before I'm just as mindless in my everyday life as I am when I model.

3
Child Bride

There's something unsettling about the fact that the main work I got between the ages of 20 and 22 was that of playing the role of a bride or a mom.

In a way, I shouldn't have been too surprised: TV shows always seem to cast 22 year olds as high school freshmen, only to cast a 29 year old as the middle-aged mother of two. It's all in a futile attempt to hide the fact that we're awkward as adolescents and wrinkly as adults; that we get a good 10 years maximum where we're not pig-faced brats or haggard old people (if we believe society, at least).

I never got that many runway gigs, and I was always passed over for jobs that needed someone to play a studious college student or a spunky young adult (ironically, those always seemed to go to the 17 year old who had flawlessly gone through puberty at the age of 10). I was too big for fashion and too offbeat for most catalogue work. But acting like someone's bride or mom was my bread and butter.

There was something peculiar about trying on wedding dresses when I was still wondering if my college boyfriend was the real deal. Much like there was something off about linking arms with a gay 19-year-old boy and pretending like we had just gotten hitched. And there was something down-

right unnerving about holding or feeding or coddling someone else's baby as if it were my own. Especially while the actual
moms—who were all old enough to have been my babysitter
back in the day—milled about on set. One minute I'm fawning
over my new legal drinking age and the next, pretend-toss-
ing a bouquet or rocking Mrs. Jenson's baby to sleep in a new
brand of cradle due out this fall.

It was all incredibly surreal. Here I was, essentially the child
bride, going up and down the fake aisle to dance music during
wedding expos and bridal shows. I felt like a princess, but the
kind of princess that people don't really talk about. I might has
well have had my father-king working behind scenes, orches-
trating the entire expo as some sort of weird type of fanfare
before he married me off to a prince from another province. A
prince who happened to be a year younger than me and very
much into guys.

So, in a way, a lot like how arranged marriages operated for
royalty in the olden days.

Granted, 20 is not exactly pre-pubescent, but when you're
an emotionally-lost college student who cannot fathom the
idea of being an adult, you might be as well be a 12-year-old
princess from a faraway land. Or a 15-year-old teen mom who
is trying to pay the bills by having pictures taken of her while
she holds her baby.

But the wedding gigs and the motherhood shoots were what
helped pay the bills, so I didn't complain. I did exactly what
was asked of me and wondered if anyone would be able to

look at the side of that highchair box or at that advertisement for a wedding boutique and wonder how the model could have ever been considered old enough for the job.

I got engaged at the tender age of 24. An age that lies somewhere between "congratulations!" and "oh God, are you pregnant?" in terms of marriage eligibility. I dove headfirst into the complex world of weddings, with gift registries and vendor meetings and wedding websites to boot.

In some weird twist of fate, as I hit my mid-twenties, the mom and bride jobs ground to a screeching halt. I continued to work with one bridal boutique—the boutique I got my own wedding dress from—but, for the most part, I was done being a child bride and mom. Most likely because I wasn't a child anymore.

I remember setting up a registry at one particular department store for my own wedding. To the right of me in the Registry Consultation Office was a picture of a bride and a groom standing in front a barn. The boy held the girl's hand with the same tentativeness as if they were out on their first date. The girl looked 18 at the absolute oldest. The boy was maybe a year older. The dress looked less like a wedding gown and more like a white prom dress. She looked sweet and carefree and obviously without a clue as to what actual weddings entail.

And maybe that's why clients want their models so young that they couldn't yet rent a car or drink. Planning a wedding is about as stressful as herding cats into single-file formation, and with roughly the same results. Being a mother is about as frustrating and exhausting and thankless as it can get. You don't want women who actually understand how the adult world works—what weddings and parenting actually entail—to model your wears. You want the spunky 20 year old who whimsically dreams of a perfect white wedding in Tahiti, or swears she knows everything there is to know about babies because she spends a few hours a week babysitting the neighbor's children. You want to draw the potential customer in with the idea that if you buy from this store, if you use this particular company's service, then maybe you'll be as happy and carefree as you think you were when you were 20.

A few years back, I ran into an old picture of me while perusing the local Babies R Us for a baby shower present. I found my mug on the side of a box for a highchair, feeding a happy baby with a serene smile on my face. The shirt was a completely different color than the one I had actually worn in the shoot, and they had photoshopped my arm, shortening it to the point that my elbow essentially stopped at my collarbone (and was made of rubber). The baby did not meet my gaze, but instead smiled blissfully at something happening off-camera. I was holding up a plastic spoon that had absolutely nothing in it.

I compared that picture to the countless other pictures on countless other boxes beside me in that store. The model moms all looked so young and energetic, like motherhood was the easiest thing in the world—at least it was now, now that they owned this new bassinet. I didn't shake my head and wonder how anyone could imagine that the girl in the picture was old enough for that baby. I simply walked away wondering why anyone would think a woman's arm could bend that way as she fed her kid in a highchair.

4

Modeling and Nudity

All right, would-be models, I'm about to lay some knowledge mulch on your garden of dreams.

(Hush. I majored in English in college. Crappy metaphors are all I have.)

Regardless, let me reveal an important little truth for you: you absolutely, positively, do not need to get naked to "make it" as a model.

To be fair, this comes with a bit more truth: you probably will not "make it" as a model in general, regardless of your foray (or lack of foraying) into nudity.

It's a gnarly little business, and a model should consider herself lucky simply if she can support herself on modeling income alone. The likelihood of a model becoming a megastar (even just within the confines of the fashion world) becomes slimmer and slimmer by the day (coincidently, at the same pace the sample sizes become slimmer and slimmer). So don't for a second think that getting naked is going to increase your chances of becoming a millionaire supermodel, because 50 x 0 still equals 0.

I should also state that there is absolutely, positively nothing wrong with nude modeling, figure modeling, and so on, and so forth. Just don't feel like you have to do it, especially when you'd rather gargle with toilet water than take off your clothing for the camera.

I had two things going for me when it came to avoiding nudity: I was primarily a commercial model (and when was the last time you saw a naked woman in an ad for lawn mowers…at least outside of Europe), and I was a teacher. Which meant that I packed a nice, powerful, one-two punch when I would get approached for nudity.

"Well, I'm a commercial model, so I wouldn't really benefit from any nude images. Oh, is that answer not good enough? How about this: I teach. I teach children. Little children. Young children. The preschool variety. Feeling oddly pedophilic now? Awesome. Glad you see things my way. I was this close to talking about changing Pull-Ups and singing the Alphabet Song."

Full disclosure: even if I were a fashion model and paid my bills by flipping burgers, I still would never have done nudity. It's not my bag. To say I'm uncomfortable with it is an understatement. I tense up in a bathing suit at photo shoots. Acting like I was raised in France in front of the camera would only result in awkward, unusable photos.

Not to mention I was raised by a set of Irish parents who were way more conservative than they'd ever care to admit, so I developed a healthy shame when it came to the human form in its most natural state.

This is one of those situations where I'm thankful I waited until I was almost 20 to model. I had no proper backbone as a teenager. I don't know how I would've handled the barrage of "offers," especially from the ones who had a hard time taking, "no," for an answer. This is how young girls end up exploited in photo shoots, but that's for another time.

Throughout the years—especially as a freelancer—I came across a lot of photographers who only had one thing on their minds. I stuck to my convictions (much to their dismay), even as some tried time and time again. And while it was frustrating, doing the modeling equivalent of, "No, you may not buy me a drink," at a bar, it did create some amusing conversations.

Example #1: To Catch a Nude Predator

Photographer: Great shoot today. You should come by the studio again soon. We could do some fine art nudes.
Me: Ah, thanks, but no thanks. I don't really do nudity.
Photographer: Aww, why not?
Whenever I think back on this conversation, I always imagine that, upon saying, "Aww, why not?", the photographer instantly transports himself in front of a white van, candy in both hands, pouting at me because I don't want to see the puppy in the back of his car.
Me: It's just not something I do. Plus, I'm a preschool teacher, and I could get fired over something like nude pictures.
The photographer more or less drops the topic and we go our separate ways. We cross paths about a year later, and it's like the

conversation had never ended.

Creepy Photographer: You really should come by the studio. We can do some fine art nudes.

Me: Nudity really isn't my thing.

Creepy Photographer: [in front of invisible van, candy in both hands] Aww, why not?

Me: Because it's just not something I do. Plus, it could be damaging for my career.

Creepy Photographer: Well we could just not...tell anybody...

"We just won't tell anybody." Well, when a photographer uses the same persuasive argument as a sexually deviant gym teacher, you know you're dealing with a stand-up guy. Why I didn't throw off my clothes and start modeling nude right then and there is beyond me.

To date, I have not run into or spoken to this particular photographer since.

Example #2: The Online Photographer Who Knows It All

Know-It-All: You would be a great addition to my portfolio. You should do a nude shoot with me.

Me: I appreciate the offer, but I don't do nudes.

Know-it-All: You're shortchanging yourself here. You really should do nudes.

Me: Again, thanks but no thanks. I don't do nudes.

Know-it-All: I hope you know you're sabotaging your career here. All the big models do nudes.

Me: I'm not looking to be a famous model. If anything, nudity would sabotage my actual career: teaching.

Know-it-All: You are so naïve. People will find out you don't do nudes and you'll lose work left and right! And then you'll have no choice but to teach!

I blocked him after that message.

For the record, I've yet to hear anyone from any agency—not my first agency, not my current agency, not any agency—warn me that I would get blacklisted for not doing nudity. In fact, every single modeling job I've had not only involved lots of clothing, but clothing and styles that were as inoffensive and nonthreatening as possible. Because this is America, and our Puritan roots keep us from selling kayaks and canoes with bare bottoms.

Example #3: The 'Old Friend' Who Has Taken Up Photography

Old college classmate: So, I hear you model!

Me: Ah, a little bit. Although not so much since I started teaching full-time.

Classmate: I got into photography recently! Mostly nature stuff, but I want to expand my portfolio.

Me: That's awesome to hear.

Classmate: You know, you could always model for me.

Me: Sure, of course. What particular genre are you looking to do? Commercial, fashion, lifestyle, portraiture…

Classmate: Nudes.

Me: Er…I don't do nudes.

Classmate: Why not?

Always with the, "Why not?" Like I'm going to respond with, "You know, I never really gave any consideration as to why. On second thought, let me take all these clothes off!"

Me: Because I'm not comfortable with it.

Classmate: Fine—what genres do you do?

Me: Commercial, fashion, lifestyle, portraiture, editorial…

Classmate: And nudes?

Me: No. Not nudes.

There was radio silence for about a month. I eventually get a new message online.

Classmate: Hey, I was curious if you still wanted to work together. My friend has a studio I can rent out. I'd love to do some interesting shots with you, maybe some nudes…

I never replied back and have yet to hear from him since.

———

Looking back, while keeping the lines of communication open made for some comical bits of dialogue, the best thing I could've done was turn and go the second they wouldn't take, "No," for an answer. If they don't listen the first time, they aren't going to listen the second (or third) time, either. And I should never have felt the need to explain myself. If I don't do a particular genre of modeling, I don't do a particular genre of modeling. I'm not kicking puppies or stealing from the UNICEF jar. I shouldn't have to defend my actions as if I were.

At the end of the day, it makes no sense to pursue someone for nude modeling so aggressively, especially since there is such a large number of figure and nude models out there. To me, it's like going after a married man or woman at the bar. You are surrounded by singles—singles who are more than ready to accept the drink of any willing patron—and yet you go after the lady who makes no attempt to hide the wedding ring on her finger. And for what? So you can have the extra satisfaction of potentially winning over someone who normally wouldn't go for that? More often than not, you're just going to end up with your drink spilled on you and a nasty reputation to precede you wherever you go.

5

The Anatomy of a Runway Mom, Case File #253

I get sent on a lot of dead-end go-sees.

These are the times when I go to a casting call or go-see and I know I'm dead in the water. Like casting calls where the client was obviously looking for the blonde party girl and I'm the brunette who looks like she's worried her library books are overdue. Or go-sees where I would stand out as the only size 6 twenty-something in a sea of size 2 teenagers. Usually, I would get sent on go-sees where they were looking for a "natural-looking girl next door" only to learn that said "girl next door" is supposed to be a larger-than-life bombshell with a narrow waist and legs that go all the way up to Canada.

One particular go-see was for a designer who was looking for size 6 girls. As a size 6 model (who had been sent on too many size 2 go-sees), I was the first to respond back and the first one there at the go-see.

Well, I was almost the first one there. Even though I had arrived way earlier than I needed to be, I was still technically second in line. I got off the elevator and saw that I would have company before the go-see began. I found a spot to stand in the hallway by the casting call room. I uttered an awkward "hello" to the model in front of me and counted the tiles to pass the time. The hallway was eerily empty: just me and the model, who was no older than 15 or 16. It was just her and me in the beginning.

Her and me and her runway mom.

Stage moms are crazed mothers who live out their failed acting dreams through their children. Pageant moms are crazed mothers who live out their failed beauty queen dreams through their children. And, in a similar vein, runway moms are crazed mothers who live out their failed modeling dreams through their children. Some people call these mothers "stage moms" as well, but I beg to differ: it is a different and special brand of cruel with mothers who drag their sons or daughters to go-see after go-see, modeling job after modeling job, prodding their children to lose more weight and be prettier, all in an effort to live out someone else's dreams of losing more weight and looking prettier.

Not all mothers of under-aged models are runway moms. I've met some incredible mothers of young models who were super sweet and sociable. These moms were clearly sources of support and guidance; moms who were there because their daughters dreamt of being a model, not because the moms dreamt of their daughters being a model. I actually got a ride home after fainting at a photo shoot by one of these kind-hearted moms (but more on that later).

However, this mom was definitely not that type of mom.

A few minutes passed. The doors to the room where the go-see would take place were still closed and I was still passing time in the hallway. I occasionally caught the eye of the young model and we would smile awkwardly at each other. The mother, on the other hand, would catch my eye and stare at me with a cold anger usually given by a queen when someone is attempting to dethrone her husband. I would reflexively give a welcoming smile, feel it quickly descend into an awkward grin, and then immediately go back to counting the tiles.

After a little while, another model came into the hallway. The young girl and I met the newcomer with a smile. The mom stared as if someone were planning a military coup against the castle.

"Is, uh, is this where the go-see is?" she asked nervously.

"Yup!" I replied a little too eagerly. The new girl took her place by one of the walls and we continued to pass the time by looking around while keeping any eye contact to an absolute minimum.

(This was long before smartphones.)

"Gorgeous day, today," I said at last.

"Yeah, it really is," said the new girl. "I love the springtime."

"How long have you been modeling?" the mom said suddenly.

Everyone else in the hallway turned and looked at the mom with the exact same expression.

"Who…me?" the new girl asked.

"Whichever," the mother responded.

"Oh, um…" the girl took a nervous swallow. "Maybe a year or so?"

The mother broke into a wicked grin.

"See, my Caylinn has been modeling since she was 10," she said. "I knew from the moment she walked around in her dress-up clothes that she was meant to be a model."

"Ah," the new girl replied.

"Y'know, I used to model, too," the mother went on. "Mostly local stuff. Never really made it big. But Caylinn, here…" The mother paused to wrap an arm around her daughter. "She has potential. I see her going places."

If I were a more vocal person, I would've said something like, "…like the therapist's office." But I kept to myself instead and thanked every possible version of God when the door to the room opened and the designer stepped out.

"Are you here for the fashion show?" she asked, as if there would be any other reason why three models and Lady Macbeth were sitting out in the hallway.

The designer led us in and showed us her wardrobe samples. Some were half-finished and still on the mannequin. Others were polished masterpieces, expertly laid out on one of the tables.

"So, I want you to try on a few of the outfits and walk for me. See what works."

The mother stepped in front of her daughter.

"You know, I noticed you only had a few models come for this," she said.

"Audition hours are until 5," the designer replied. "I'm sure more will come in later."

"But, y'know…" the mother pressed. "I could always try on a few pieces for you. You never know. I might be what you're looking for, for the show. Two children later and I still have my girlish figure."

The designer pressed her lips together and sighed.

"Let's focus on the models, first," she offered.

The designer handed each of us two outfits. There were no closed-off areas to change into, so we all turned our backs to each other and began the awkward outfit-change ritual that any modest model who has ever been in runway shows knows all too well.

I maneuvered out of my jeans as part of my little dance to keep me as much clothed as I could possibly be. I reached for the dress and stepped my feet through the top section. I was already prepping myself for the move where I remove my shirt, only to have it immediately replaced with the dress's top (a move that I had perfected with time and, in some weird way, am actually quite proud of). But a jarring stop of the dress snapped me out of my song-and-dance reverie.

I looked down to examine the dress and found that the form-fitting dress stopped fitting my form just above my knees. I tried crossing my legs, bending my knees, praying my thighs would become narrower, but nothing worked. The dress was going nowhere faster than a coke fiend's future.

I didn't want to draw too much attention to the fact that my size 6 physique was mysteriously not fitting into a size 6 dress. I shimmied off the dress and reached for the second one, already annoyed that my underwear had been on quasi-public display for way longer than my little routine usually allows.

I looked at the second dress and felt a bit more optimistic. It was form-fitting at the torso, but with a zipper in the back and a flowing skirt for the bottom half. I unzipped the dress, stepped in, and resumed the dance until the sleeves of the dress were on both shoulders.

I want to say, "comfortably on both shoulders," but there was nothing comfortable about how this dress felt. The shoulder width of the dress was a solid inch or two narrower than my own shoulder width. I could barely move my arms outside of an awkward set of movements that I call, "The Zombie Who Gave Up On Life…Again." I wiggled my arms in stilted, awkward circles until my hands could finally reach my back. I fumbled for the zipper, hoping that everything would shift into place as soon as I zipped up the dress.

This was when I learned that the zipper edges were not on my back per se, so much as they were along the sides of my torso. I would've had a better shot closing the wealth gap in America or negotiating an Israeli-Palestinian truce than bringing the two sides of the zipper anywhere close to meeting.

With no more outfits to try on, I turned to the designer to admit defeat.

"I can't seem to zip this dress up," I stated dumbly.

(Y'know, since, "These dresses are making me feel like a fat-ass," seemed in poor taste.)

The runway mom looked up with a deliriously gleeful look on her face. The designer came over, crossed her arms, and shook her head.

"What size are you?" the designer asked.

"Um, a 6?" I replied.

Part of me wanted to say: "You caught me. I'm a size 22, hoping you would take pity on me and redesign your entire collection to fit my frame." But, as is the theme with me, I kept quiet.

"Really," the designer went on as if she didn't believe me. "These should fit a size 6."

I bit my tongue.

"In children's? Because yeah, I see these fitting a size 6 in children's."

"I don't know," I said, shrugging as best as I could with my shoulders still in the woolen vise grip. "But I am a size six. My measurements are 35-27-37."

The designer cocked an eyebrow.

"My dresses will not fit someone with measurements like that."

"Gee—you think? I can't believe you are wasting your talent making clothes when your deduction skills could solve murders around the world."

"Oh."

Not knowing what else to say to her, I simply peeled myself out of the dress, reversing the dance until my shirt and jeans were properly back on. Part of me wanted to roll the waist of my jeans back, pull out the tag, and say, "Look at that number! Tell me that's not a pair of size 6 jeans!"

But I didn't.

"Let me try those on," the mother called out before I could even place the second dress back on the table.

The designer sighed and rolled her eyes.

"Go right ahead, then," the designer replied.

"You know, I used to model, too." The mother stripped down to her underwear and marched across the room. She grabbed the first dress with so much gusto that the fabric hit me in the arm. "Mostly local stuff. I see my daughter going places, though. Really going places. Although I don't mind dabbling in modeling still. You're never too old to appreciate fashion!"

I grabbed my bag and left before the runway mom could put on the first dress. Much to my chagrin, the two other models fit into their outfits like it was made for them. The teenaged girl looked elegant in a long, draping gown and the second model was putting the finishing touches on a mini-dress with glittered edges that fit her like a glove. A glitter-edged glove, but a glove all the same.

Perhaps they had received a different email. Or perhaps they went in thinking they were too small, but hoped that somehow the outfits would fit, or that the designer would alter them. It didn't matter: once again I was the "big model" surrounded by girls who were the perfect fit.

I exited the building and downright poured out onto the sidewalk. I looped around to one of the side streets, intentionally taking a circuitous route back to the train station. I waited for the train with my teeth clenched and my feet tapping. When it arrived, I boarded my train and collapsed into my seat with my head hung back.

You have to have a thick skin in this industry, but that day, my skin felt thicker than usual. Everything felt thicker. It took a long train ride back home before I could fully process what had happened. And it took a bit of retrospection (read: dwelling) before I felt the wind come back into my sails.

Yes, I looked like an idiot in front of the designer, and I definitely didn't get the runway gig. But not getting the job also meant I would not have to see the Runway Mom again if I didn't want to. And heaven knows she probably spent the entire show telling everyone backstage: "I used to model, too, y'know. I almost modeled for this show as well. I still have in it me, you know. I could still model if I wanted to. But my daughter, she's going places. She's going to be a star."

6

Hey, Let's Talk About That Time I Fainted at a Photo Shoot

Hey, let's talk about that time I fainted at a photo shoot.

I'm not proud of it. At the time of this publication, I have been modeling for 8 years. I have been alive for 27. And it is still considered one of the Top 10 Most Embarrassing Things I Have Ever Done. A list that includes such wonderful gems as puking in the stairwell of my junior high and answering the phone by making a crude inside joke, only to realize that it wasn't my friend who had called but the woman I babysat for.

Oh, and temporarily going unconscious while waiting in line outside an Old Country Buffet ("waiting in line outside an Old Country Buffet" in general is on that list as well), but that is for another time.

It was no one's fault but my own. I was sick as a dog, but refused to cancel on a shoot. I looked pallid and in a slight amount of pain, but, dammit, a commitment was a commitment and I am stubborn. I simply did my job and retreated to my sickness survival kit in between sets. I downed enough vitamin C to make an orange grove feel inadequate. I sipped on enough chicken noodle soup to keep Campbell's in business on my patronage alone. And I chugged water like I could flood the flu out of me.

We changed wardrobes and hair/make-up styles three times, culminating in a vintage look complete with a tea cup/saucer combo and a TIME magazine from the 1960s. In a way, my pale, slightly miserable face was exactly what such a shoot needed. I looked exactly as outraged as I needed to be when the other model fake-whispered something in my ear. I looked exactly as taken-back as I needed to be when I pretended to read about JFK's assassination. And I looked exactly as disinterested as I needed to be when I narrowed my eyes and focused on the teacup in front of me.

Six hours, three wardrobe styles, and two location changes later, the photographer called it a wrap.

And like that, I hit the floor.

It was like one of those stories where a dying man or an elderly lady fight to stay alive long enough so they can see their child get married, or so they can enjoy one last Christmas with their family. It was exactly like that, only instead of dying, it was passing out, and instead of a daughter's wedding or holidays with the family, it was an unpaid modeling job.

I sat up almost as quickly as I had fallen down, hoping to pass off the fainting spell as a slip or a spill. I attempted to stand back up, only to reel forward onto my hands and knees.

The make-up artist wasted no time tending to my post-collapsed state. She helped me up, giving instructions to everyone around her like she was an ER doctor. With her support, I made my way to a nearby seat and slumped against the adjacent table. After a few sips of a soda (and a few dry heaves), I started feeling a little better. The mother of the other model gave me a ride back to my dorm, where I finally admitted defeat and spent the rest of the weekend in bed.

When I tell this story to people, the first response is almost always same: "Did you have enough to eat?"

Which, if we're being honest here, is a thinly veiled way of saying, "Were you starving yourself?"

Yes, I was starving myself. I was fulfilling the modeling dream of living off of diet coke, full-calorie cocaine, and dreams of superstardom. Never mind the part where I was eating soup by the metric ton and drinking enough fizzy vitamin C drinks to make a healthy person want to vomit. Pointing to starvation as the cause makes as much sense as pointing to the vitamin C.

But maybe that's it. Maybe I hadn't fainted. Maybe I had overdosed. Maybe there's a dark underbelly to the vitamin world, where people overdose on magnesium tablets in dark, dingy basements. Where the FDA neglects to tell you that enough vitamin C will render you comatose. And—God bless my resiliency—I only reacted by temporarily going unconscious.

I'm a survivor story. Where's my million-dollar book deal and motivational speaking tour, huh?

Cut to two years later. I was working a bridal show in a small town in New Hampshire. Me and three other models were fulfilling our job requirements by smiling on pedestals for all the would-be brides to see. We changed positions around the room, going from pedestal to pedestal every fifteen minutes. We did a few rotations in this manner before sneaking into a small bathroom off to the side for a quick gown change (and you haven't lived until you've done the "nobody sees me unclothed" dance with a 30-pound wedding gown). We returned to the pedestals and repeated the process.

The job took an ugly turn as the expo wound down. The expo coordinator asked us to remain on the pedestals, even as the guests were ushered away from the vendors' area. An hour ticked slowly by as we stood on what were starting to feel like little squares of death; all the while the expo participants sat at the tables across the room, ate meals from the local catering company, and listened intently as a local wedding planner listed all the different ways brides can spend their money on their wedding day. We shifted from foot to foot. We surreptitiously slipped off our high-heeled shoes. The bridal boutique's owner came over and apologized profusely for the lack of communication (and common sense) on the part of the expo coordinator. We humbly accepted the apology and stared at the meals being served across the room, wondering if we'd ever get down and eat as well.

As a second wedding planner came to the podium to talk to the guests, one of the models asked if she could take a break from her pedestal. The owner of the gown company helped her down and the model-bride made her way to one of the vendor tables. Before the wedding planner on the other end of the room could finish her speech about care baskets in bathrooms, we all heard a loud thunk. We turned and found the model-bride with her back on the floor.

People from the other side of the vendor table rushed over to help her. Guests at the dining tables stood up to gawk. The expo coordinator came up to the remaining models and said, "You guys can go home now."

I had planned to get a ride back to the city with the now-downed model, and, in light of what had just transpired, I was no longer her passenger so much as I was her chaperone, there to take the wheel in case a second fainting spell hit. When she swore she felt good enough to drive, we boarded her Jeep and made our way back to Boston.

"I can't believe I fainted!" she said as soon as we left the parking lot.

"We were standing in those heavy dresses for quite some time," I replied, the green expanse of New Hampshire rushing by me. I sipped on the Diet Coke I got for free from one of the vendors and carefully monitored the model for any signs of light-headedness.

"But still—I can't believe I fainted!" she went on. "How embarrassing!"

"If it's anything," I offered. "I know how it feels."

7

I Got Mine Where You Got Yours

Being a "curvy" model has almost always worked to my detriment.

As the talent director at my first agency once warned me, I would have a hard time finding work because I had a large bosom and bigger-than-average gluteus maximus.

Or, as she put it: "Because you're all this and all this," as she grabbed her boobs and her butt.

Which might be why I got as much work as I did pretending to be a mother. Nothing says, "fertile adult" quite like a college sophomore with a D cup.

But, usually, I played down my curves as much as possible during go-sees. I wore a lot of black and replaced my regular bra with a sports one. I prayed that the people in charge of the go-see would ignore my measurements and be wowed by my incredible model-like presence instead.

This has yet to happen, but I am still holding out hope.

When I was 22, my then-agency sent me out to an audition for a commercial. I knew nothing about what the commercial would entail, or what the commercial was even for. All I knew was that the models needed to wear a tank top to the casting call. I found my best bosom-downplaying top and went on my merry way.

I was the first of two girls to arrive for the casting. The man in charge of the studio took our names and our comp cards and passed out a two-paged script. He then brought us to a grey backdrop and sat us down behind a camera.

"Just look over the script a little bit while I get everything set," he told us.

I scanned through the script as the man fiddled with the lighting and the camera. In the scene, I (or the girl next to me) would be a nurse, sitting at the bar section of a diner. I (or the girl next to me) would be a construction worker who approaches Girl #1 and asks her where she got "them." Girl #2 would point to Girl #1's chest area when saying, "them." Girl #2 would then look down at her chest and go, "Well, I got mine, the same place you got yours."

At the end of the scene, you learn just what the girls are talking about: uniforms. Scrubs, construction vests, and the like. All sorts and varieties of work uniforms—all available at this particular store.

I couldn't help by chuckle. Oh, you thought we meant our boobs? Silly, we meant our outfits! It all wrapped up nicely with the commercial's ending: one of us would look at a steak meal being brought out of the diner's kitchen and go, "Nice tips."

Ah, innuendos. They never get old.

The guy behind the camera asked if we were ready. He assigned us our roles (I was the nurse; she was the construction worker) and, like a proper director, yelled, "Action!"

We did our best to deliver the lines. In that moment, I developed an intense sympathy for the actors in low-budget commercials; the ones who awkwardly shuffle up to the camera and deliver their lines like they are being held at gunpoint. There was absolutely nothing natural about placing my fingertips just under my collarbone and saying, "Well, I got mine the same place you got yours."

I mean, honestly—how would I know where she got her uniform? And maybe she's not a construction worker at all. Maybe she had robbed a construction worker and ran off with his hardhat. And who goes up to a nurse to ask where she got "them" anyway? If I ever saw a nurse hunched over the bar section of a diner, I'd assume she had just finished an 18-hour shift. If I am to do anything, it is going to be sending a cup of coffee her way, not asking her where she purchases her scrubs.

But, regardless, we made it to the end of the script, both of us looking at up the director-casting-man for our next move.

"That's good, that's good, but, uh … can we be a little less … friendly?" he said to me. "Try slowing down your speech. Don't be afraid to have your hand linger on your—uh—chest."

We tried again, my right hand still by my collarbone as if my ribs were made of hot coals. I slowed down my delivery, gave the camera knowing smirks, and hit the last page one more time. I breathed out a, "Nice tips," and waited until the camera was good and off before I rolled my eyes.

The director guy paused for a moment after turning off the camera. He sighed and looked at me like I was a four-year-old trying to read a picture book.

"Let's try that one more time," he said at last.

It was quite clear that the director wanted the models to deliver their lines like sex phone operators. Slow and low and filled to the brim with innuendo and repressed lust. The problem was that I was delivering the lines like a Back to School commercial for the local department store. With each take, I felt more and more empathy for the girls who did the chat line commercials after midnight. What is sexy about saying words someone else thought up, in a room with a thousand bright lights and a ton of strangers, and into something as lifeless as a camera lens?

The director thanked us for our time after the fourth or fifth take. He ushered me out and paused to chat a little more with the girl next to me: a girl whose bust could have made Pamela Anderson reconsider her life choices. Compared to her, I was exactly the un-curvy girl that I pretended to be at go-sees. Compared to her, I didn't need to wear sports bras. I could walk in with my best push-up bra, my most revealing top, and a neon arrow pointing directly at my mammary region, and I would still pale in comparison.

If I had gotten mine from the same place where she had gotten hers, I would've stormed back to said place and demanded a full refund, because I had obviously been swindled.

I didn't get the job, which surprised exactly no one. I kept my eye out for the commercial, especially on shows that aired after 10 p.m. But I had no such luck. I was curious as to who they eventually casted and how the commercial turned out. I wanted to meet these girls and shake their hands. I wanted to congratulate whoever could effortlessly point to her chest, stare seductively into the camera, and say: "Well, I got mine from the same place you got yours."

8

How to Lose a Model in Two Emails or Less

Photographers (and would-be photographers) take note: this is how you lose a model that has already signed on to do a photo shoot with you.

Sometime in 2009, I had a photo shoot set up with a local photographer. It was nothing too spectacular: the shoot was a simple collaborative effort in order to improve on our respective portfolios. We had the date, the details, and the location all pinned down.

And then: I ate pavement.

I can't even explain why I fell the way I did or why the wound took on a weird scrape-bruise hybrid, but my chin was now home to the type of injury you'd expect to see on a boxer after a sparring session gone horribly wrong.

Since my timing has always been impeccable, I took said spill just days before the photo shoot. I emailed the photographer, explaining my situation, hoping to reschedule.

"I'm sorry to hear that you got injured," he wrote back. "How bad is it? Is it something we can cover up with makeup?"

"It's big and glaring," I said in my reply email, attempting to make light of a pretty ugly situation. "It's like an abrasion and a bruise all rolled into one. You could call it an abruision, or a bruisasion. Really, there is no other way to describe it other than it looks like my chin got a hickey from a brick."

The photographer replied back with one simple line:

"Well, if I were the one giving you a hickey, it wouldn't just be on your chin."

Spoiler alert: the photo shoot never happened.

9

The Anatomy of a Runway Mom, Case File #17,603

I first met Mrs. Burnout during a go-see for a fashion show.

I call her Mrs. Burnout because that's exactly what she looked like: someone who had lived hard and fast for the first 30 years of her life, only to crash and burn and meander through the remaining years. She had a look on her face that one only gets when they had squandered their youth by partying (or cage fighting).

The show itself was simple enough: a few fashion design students from a college in Boston were hosting a runway show as part of a larger charity event. The event was happening in Middle of Nowhere, Massachusetts. I had already worked with one of the designers and was more than happy to jump in.

Since I was already going to work for the designers, the go-see for the show was a more or less a formality. So much of a formality that we actually drove out of Boston together, talking about the show and the agency in western Massachusetts and what we could expect. We talked about how Bostonians never really venture out of the 495 Belt—a nice little loop around Boston, with a radius of roughly 30 miles and

Interstate 495 serving as guard and gatekeeper. As far as any egocentric Bostonian was concerned, civilization lived inside that loop, and Thar-Be-Dragons lived outside of it (unless you were going on vacation).

We drove out past the 495 Belt, past Worcester, and into the great unknown. We pulled off the highway, into a small town that none of us had heard of, and followed the road until it led us to a tiny, off-white ranch house located across the street from a strip mall.

At the end of the driveway stood a sign for the agency. We'll call this agency The Haha We Took Your Child's Money Agency, because I get the feeling that that was only way this particular agency made any money in the first place. The sign for Haha We Took Your Child's Money Agency was the same type used for the "Single? (insertregionhere)-singles.com" signs that litter the sides of most major roads. It was nothing more than a flimsy piece of plastic held in place by two metal spokes. The graphics were jarring, with enough pink bubbles and purple glitter text to drive even the most hardcore Lisa Frank fanatic mad. We followed the arrow at the bottom of the sign and looped around back, where we found a walkout basement with a similar sign stapled to the basement's door.

One of the designers cautiously knocked. The door immediately flung open. On the opposite side of the doorframe stood a 40-something female with perfectly quaffed hair and an air about her that let you know that she was once a model. Or beauty pageant contestant. Or both.

"Come in, come in!" The former pageant queen/model stepped back and ushered us inside. "You must be the designers!"

We stepped into what would've normally been a nice finished basement. Only instead of old posters and sports memorabilia, there were white-framed snapshots of high school girls lining the walls. Instead of a sectional sofa, there was a metal desk pushed up against the wall by the door. Instead of a television set, there was a set of camera lights in one corner, all held up by PVC pipes that still had the Home Depot stickers on them.

"I can't wait for you to meet our models," the woman said, gesturing to the cluster of 20 metal chairs on the opposite side of the room. Scattered amongst the chairs was a set of 9 or 10 girls who looked no older than the girls in the snapshots. Most had a distant, distracted look about them, as if they were waiting to see their doctor. Most of the girls were alone. One girl was off to the side, sitting with her legs and arms crossed in the way that only bored, annoyed teenaged girls could do. Beside her was a middle-aged woman with a face that had been through a few city miles and a smile to match. She was flipping through a black portfolio book, whispering things to the angsty teenager in rapid-fire succession.

Ladies and gentlemen, I present to you: Mrs. Burnout.

"So, let's try on a few outfits, shall we?" the pageant woman beamed.

We walked into the second room of the basement, which

looked identical to the first, only with more lights tied onto makeshift stands and a few card tables in the center of the room. The designers laid out their wears and started dividing up the models. I stood by the designer I knew and passed the time by straightening the outfits on the table.

"And, uh, are you a designer, too?" the agency/pageantry lady asked.

"Oh, no, I'm actually a model," I replied.

"A model?" the lady repeated with a look that most mean girls can only dream of one day mastering.

I stood up a little straighter and smiled.

"Yes, I've actually already worked with Tina," I said, gesturing to the designer talking to the teenaged girls. "She's the one who had called me to model for the show."

"I see. I assumed only my girls would be doing this show," she said, rolling her eyes like I couldn't inconvenience her more if I tried.

I shrugged in response.

"Well, then," the lady said with a snarled smile. "The more the merrier, I guess."

The lady turned away from me and tended to the other models in the room. I took a long, uncertain breath and continued to help with the selection process.

Since there were so few models for the show, most of the girls would be working with multiple designers, switching out of their wears as fast as possible before going on stage again. The girls tried on almost every design that was brought in, moving around until the designers felt they had found a good fit. Mrs. Burnout scuttled around behind her daughter, tugging at the outfits until they looked the way she wanted them to look. She continued speaking in hushed words to her daughter, which seemed to go in one ear and out the other.

The models were picked, the outfits were assigned, and we were good to go for the show. The show—as well as the Haha We Took Your Child's Money Agency and the mom who looked like she was one new hangover away from a complete breakdown – dropped from immediate thought until that following Saturday.

We drove out a second time to Thar-Be-Dragons, Massachusetts, this time to a small function hall in the center of town. I breathed a sigh of relief, as the mean girl/former model/former pageant contestant agency director was nowhere to be found. But the mother of the bored teen mom was there, still fiddling with her daughter's hair, still looking perpetually hungover.

"If you would just use the hair treatment I got you, you wouldn't have all these split ends," I heard her say when I took a seat next to them.

"Mom," her daughter huffed, her lips barely moving. "I'm not putting animal placenta in my hair."

"Then you are just going to have to have split ends for the rest of your life," Mrs. Burnout replied, dropping the hair as if it were infected. "I hope you can live with yourself."

The bored teenager rolled her eyes and looked away. After a few minutes, one of the designers came in.

"We finally have a room ready for hair and makeup," she said. "They can work on you guys four at a time and rotate out until everyone is ready."

Mrs. Burnout wasted no time in leading her daughter first into the room. Before the rest of us could even set our stuff down, Mrs. Burnout marched over to the row of chairs and set her daughter down in the one closest to the hairstylists.

"So, I can start on her makeup." A lady to the side of Mrs. Burnout's daughter stepped forward. "Then Brittany can work on her hair when—."

"No, no, no," Mrs. Burnout interrupted. "I need you to work on her hair first. I don't want her makeup getting smudged because of the incompetence of the hairstylist."

The hairstylists behind the chair stayed remarkably silent.

"We always do touchups before the show," the makeup artist offered.

"Not good enough. Touchups are just that: touchups. Not for major mistakes," Mrs. Burnout countered. "Now, for my daughter's hair, I was thinking a very intricate updo. Braids on this side, loops on this side…"

"The designers have actually picked out what styles they want their models to have," one hairstylist piped in with extra force.

"Oh." Mrs. Burnout eyed the hairstylist before crossing her arms. "Well, then. Looks like I'm not needed here." She gave her daughter the once over and dropped her voice an octave. "However: if she doesn't look like the supermodel she is when I get back, you will not hear the end of it from me. Mark my word."

Mrs. Burnout spun her heels and marched out of the room. The rest of us slowly walked over to the makeup artists and hairstylists, sitting in the seats like we were afraid of rigging a booby trap.

For a while, we all just sat there in silence, eyeing the floor while we either got prepped or waited our turn. Sometime after the make-up artists and hairstylists finished their work on their first models and moved on to a different model sitting in the prep chairs, one of the more brazen models turned to the daughter of Mrs. Burnout.

"Is she always like that?" she asked.

"Who?" asked Mrs. Burnout's daughter.

"Your mom."

The girl rolled her eyes and nodded—or nodded as best as she could while getting her hair done.

"Isn't it the worst?" Mrs. Burnout's daughter noted. "It's honestly like this every day."

"Sheesh," the second model replied. "Sorry about that."

"Like, she tried to get me on one of those cyan pepper cleanses before this show. Told me I still had a few more pounds to lose," Mrs. Burnout's daughter continued. "When I refused, suddenly every meal she made has cyan pepper in it. Like that's going to do anything."

"Moms can be the worst sometimes," another girl noted.

"She's, like, way too into this modeling thing," she continued. "She'll honestly text me in the middle of class about go-sees and what have you. She's even told me to skip school for them."

"Wow. Just…wow."

"As she puts it, 'education can wait; the window to superstardom is limited.' Whatever that means." The daughter paused for a second as the hairstylist gently tilted her head to the other side. "I mean, she is up my ass about picking a college in New York, or LA…wherever I can 'be a star' or whatever." The girl sighed and looked down at her lap. "I just want to be a vet or something."

"Your hair is done, sweetie," said the hairstylist after a while. "You can wait over there until the show starts."

We rotated around the small group of hairstylists and makeup artists, each getting our turn for hair and makeup. The designers came in soon after and started dressing everyone for the show. As if she could sense a disturbance in the force, Mrs. Burnout stormed back in, still looking as much like a washed-up celebrity as any of the washed-up celebrities on reality TV right now.

"How does my superstar look?" she cooed out, her eyes scanning the room.

"Just fine, Mom," said a voice in the back corner.

Mrs. Burnout edged her way over to the rolling racks of clothing, pushing a few of the racks out of the way so she could get a clearer view of her daughter.

"What is this!" Mrs. Burnout yelped.

Tina, the designer I knew, came over to see what was the matter.

"You call this okay?" Mrs. Burnout used one hand to point to Tina and the other to point to her daughter. "Look at this!"

Tina peered over and shrugged her shoulders.

"She looks great," she said. "I don't get the problem."

"The problem is it's generic," Mrs. Burnout hissed. "She looks just like all the other models!"

"That's kind of the idea," Tina replied. "Same uniform look. The emphasis is on the clothing, anyway."

"The emphasis should be on the models," said Mrs. Burnout. "Specifically, this model. How is she supposed to stand out when she looks like everyone else?"

"I'm sure you'll find a way," Tina countered.

The comment had either left Mrs. Burnout speechless or motivated her to actually come up with a plan. Either way, Mrs. Burnout stormed out of the room for a second time. We didn't see her again until right before the show, when she situated herself backstage. She fiddled with her daughter's first set of clothing, surreptitiously pulling down a few strands from the updo until the daughter had a distinctly more edgy look than the rest of us. She stood guard over the changing area during the show, undressing her daughter when it was time to switch wardrobes and attempting with each wardrobe change to move her daughter to the front of the line.

Even with the chaos going on backstage, the show was over before we knew it and we were all back in the dressing room, changing back into our regular clothes, ready to call it a night.

"Are you guys doing any photo shoots soon?" Mrs. Burnout asked. "Especially for any magazines or such?"

"Um, we might…" said Tina.

"If so, my daughter would be a perfect fit, literally and figuratively. And she's already proven her X factor with this show.

Here…" Mrs. Burnout reached into her purse and pulled out a business card. "Here is all the contact info you need. Let's stay in touch."

"Uh, sure…" Tina scanned the room before giving a wavering smile. "I'll keep you in mind."

Mrs. Burnout proceeded to give the rest of the designers her business card before returning her attention to her daughter. She ruffled her daughter's hair, tsk-tsked at the split ends, and led her out of the room without so much as a, "Good-bye," to the other models.

This was the first time I really recognized the reality about the children of Runway Moms. This was not a girl who was going to grow up and become a superstar. This was a girl who was going to grow up and resent her mom for pushing modeling on her over every other aspect in her life. I spent the car ride back to Boston imagining just what Mrs. Burnout's daughter would do once she graduated high school.

I'd like to pretend that she got accepted to a tier-1 school, maybe somewhere in Chicago or Seattle, far away from her mom. I'd like to think she went on to study veterinary science—or quantum physics, or molecular biology. And I'd also like to think that she'd return home for holidays and have an extra helping of mashed potatoes while she discussed the academic world, if only to spite the woman who had her blood-shot eyes set on the catwalk.

10

We're Confident In Your Inability to Measure Yourself

Those who have gone through the joys of purchasing a traditional wedding dress can understand this frustration. For those who haven't, let me break down what happens when you go dress shopping:

Upon finding The Dress, your measurements are taken and they order your gown. The gown comes in, the seamstress makes any necessary alterations, and then you must keep those exact measurements from that very moment until your wedding day; never gaining or losing weight, lest you stop fitting into a very unforgiving bodice.

Now, imagine being that way, only replace, "from the fitting until your wedding day" with, "forever."

Being a model means that everyone who even potentially wants to hire you already knows your measurements. And your measurements cannot change. Even temporarily. I had the misfortune once of doing an intensive elliptical exercise right before a fitting. Anyone who knows anything about exercise knows that muscles tend to swell after being strained. And, as much as we joke about the gluteal region, they are still muscles. Muscles that can swell up a lot if you've been, say, working the elliptical at Level 10 for the last 45 minutes. As a result, my hip measurements were a solid inch bigger than what my agency said my measurements were—something that one of the designers kept bringing up over and over and over again, ironically making me feel about [this] big in this process.

I don't believe in lying about my measurements because I like not being known as that model who lies about her measurements. No one is going to bring in a model who says she has a 24" waist, find out she actually has a 28" waist, and still keep her on because she's just so spunky. When asked for my dress size, I always give a range as well as my measurements (with a friendly reminder that sizes are about as consistent as the numbers in pi when it comes to various department stores).

Back when I freelanced, I landed a pretty nice role in an advertising video. The video would never make it to TV, but it would make its rounds to various head honchos in major companies. I met with the coordinators, who asked for my dress size. As was my standard, I gave them my size range, as well as my measurements, noting which stores considered me a size 6 and which stores considered me a size 8. They told me they would go out and find the outfits they wanted for the shoot, and I would come by and try them on beforehand.

A week later, I came in and found a rack filled with clothes. Dresses and skirts and blouses galore. I was ecstatic, as part of my payment was the wardrobe itself (the other part being a somewhat modest paycheck). I went in for the fitting, excited for all the cool soon-to-be-office wear I was about to receive.

I tried on a skirt that was supposed to rest at my waist and watched as it fell to my hips. I changed out of the skirt and into a dress that so wide that I didn't need to unzip it to put it on. I put on a pair of pants that had enough room in them for another hipbone and a half. I looked at the size tags: every-thing was at least a size 10, if not bigger.

"Hey," I said, meekly poking out of the bathroom I was using as a changing room, "all these items seem to be a bit big on me."

"Oh, what sizes are they?" one of the coordinators asked, as if magical elves had bought the outfits instead of the people in charge.

"Well, this one is a size 10, and I think some of these are a 12," I answered.

"Oh, well, we didn't want to take any chances," the coordinator explained, obviously not surprised at my answer. "We figured it was better for items to be a bit loose and clip them back than to have them not fit in the first place."

Great. I'll just make sure to invest in a ton of clips when I wear these pants in real life.

"We'll be getting a few other outfits before the shoot, just to round things out," the coordinator continued. Round things out—unlike what my hips are doing in these pants. "What size are you again?"

"I'm typically a 6, although sometimes I'm an 8, depending on the store," I explained for the tenth time. "But, really, I am never any bigger than a size 8. I have a 27" waist and 38" hips. That might help in making the selection."

"Well, good to know," said the coordinator with a voice usually saved for a toddler who tells you that he's going to be a superhero when he grows up.

Two days later, I arrived on set for the marketing commercial. I was ushered in to the back room, where they worked on my hair and makeup while showing me the final picks for the shoot.

"So, we decided on this black dress, this blouse-and-skirt combo, and this pantsuit," a second coordinator told me as she pulled out the items. Aside from the blouse and skirt, everything was brand new. After getting my hair and makeup done, I tried on the new outfits. The pants fell to my ankles and I was downright swimming in the back dress.

I checked the size of the pants: 12. I checked the size of the dress: 14.

"There's a small problem," I said to the second coordinator. "Well, the opposite of small, really: this dress is a 14."

"Yes, and?"

I swiveled my hips. The dress responded by making hypnotic waves as it swirled across my torso.

"It's just—uh— a bit big on me," I explained, doing my best not to sound like a prima donna who was given club soda instead of seltzer.

"We figured that would be the case," said the second coordinator, downright parroting what the first coordinator had said earlier. "We decided it was better to err on the side of big and avoid any embarrassing situations at the shoot."

Yes, because that is way more embarrassing than a model with her pants by her ankles.

I was pinned and clipped into place, with an explicit warning to never turn my side or my back to the camera. I did the best with what I had and gave my most convincing "you should buy this shit!" smile into the camera and sighed inwardly when the director said it was a wrap.

I went into the back room, unclipped my clothing, and allowed the pants from the pantsuit to fall back down to my ankles. I gave my actual jeans a hug and a quiet thank you for fitting my frame. I put on my own shirt, mumbling something akin to religious prayer.

Hail cotton, full of strands, the shirt shall fit thee.

"Great shoot," said the head of the film company after I had changed. "If there is anything from the wardrobe that you'd want, let me know. It's all yours if you'd like." He said this as if this had not been the agreed-upon compensation; like he had just had a moment of altruism and suddenly decided he wanted to be just like Oprah.

You get a shirt, and you get a shirt. This whole room gets a poorly fitting shirt.

"That's very, uh, gracious of you," I responded. "But I think I'll be set. Thank you, though."

I left that shoot, stewing in my own frustration as I waited for the train to arrive. I wasn't sure what bothered me more: the fact that I was walking away with only half of my payment, or the fact that the people in charge repeatedly assumed I was lying about my measurements. Even when they saw me try on outfits that could've fit two of me inside, they swore I wasn't the size that they thought I was. In my eyes, they had assumed I was yet another airhead model, too stupid to know what her actual size was, or too conniving to tell the truth.

The only thing that brought a smile to my face during my commute back home was the image of me taking the entire wardrobe and wearing said items to my internship. I imagined me walking up and down the corridors of the publishing firm wearing a size 14 dress with five industrial clips holding everything in place. I imagined me having to sit on the edge of my seat in a meeting because one of the butterfly clips kept digging into the back of the chair. I imagined the looks I would get from my superiors, and I imagined me laughing off their concerns, telling them that I was simply erring on the side of big. Because wouldn't that be embarrassing otherwise.

11

A Face Meant for No Screen

I'll be the first to admit that I am not an actress. I never did drama in high school and never so much as took a theatre class in college. The closest I've come to "acting" was when I participated in a few 48-hour film challenges, where everyone pitched in, worked for free, and, really, nobody ever saw my stupid little film (or my stupid little acting skills).

I got an opportunity when I first started modeling to audition for the role of the "mean/ditzy model" for a movie that they never revealed the name of. I decided to give it a go, since I really had nothing to lose. The casting director gave me a time and place to audition and told me to bring in a photo of myself.

I arrived at the auditions, a little 8 x 6 photo that I had received for free from my very first photo shoot in hand. I signed in at the door and was soon approached by a man with a large binder in the crook of his elbow and glasses with impossibly thick frames on his face.

"And you are?" he said, angling the binder away from him.

"Um, Abby?" I replied daftly. "I have an audition…" I fingered the 8 x 6 snapshot and attempted to meet the eyes of the guy, but he was already scanning over the papers clipped to the front of his binder.

"Ah, yes, hi...Abby." He opened his binder and thumbed over a few pages before pulling out a stapled set of 8. "You'll be auditioning for the role of Alexis. She's supposed to be a bit self-absorbed, very in-your-face and sarcastic. But ditzy and airheaded as well." He took his eyes off of the binder just long enough to hand over my portion of the script. "Your parts are highlighted. I'll let you know when you're up."

I walked over to a sleek set of couches and sat down, script and snapshot in my lap. To my left was a petite girl with sur-realistically tiny waist and arms. In her lap was a leather port-folio with an 8 x 10 professional headshot resting on top of it. She saw me staring at her picture and smiled broadly, obvi-ously having zero qualms about her image being on display. I scanned the room and saw that almost everyone had some variation of a leather portfolio and 8 x 10 headshot.

"This is my third audition here, actually. And that's just this week," I overheard one guy say to the would-be actor next to him. "Did you hear back about that Kevin James movie, by the way?"

It was at that exact moment that I realized just how out of my league I was. Here I was, with a free 8 x 6 picture and not much else on my lap, surrounded by people who did this for a living. Everyone looked like they could step on set at any moment and steal the scene. I felt painfully average and unremarkable next to these people. It was like going to a Halloween party wearing cat ears and normal clothing as my "costume", only to realize that everyone else came dressed in elaborate outfits.

Although any person who is so unadventurous as to wear cat ears and call it a costume deserves that type of upstaging. Weirdly, that bit of information wasn't very comforting for me at that moment.

I did my best to ignore the pit forming in my stomach and I forced my eyes back down at the script. I went over the lines repeatedly, mouthing the words and imagining how Alexis, the self-absorbed, slightly ditzy, very sarcastic, in-your-face-but-airheaded-small-part-in-a-feature-length-film would say them. In the end, I found myself alternating between exaggerating the lines past the point of any believability and saying the lines as a vaguely modified version of myself.

I doubted either would win me the role.

"Abby?" The bespectacled man approached, his binder now held against his chest with one arm. "You're up."

"Thank you," I said, nearly folding my photo in half. I got up and walked through the double doors and into a completely sparse room, save for two sets of tables, with four or five people sitting behind them.

"And you are…Abby?"

Nope. I'm Elvis and I've just entered the building.

"Yup, that's me."

"Great. I'll take your photo and we can get started."

I handed over my completely unprofessionally-sized professional picture, doing my best to keep my limbs from locking up as I did so. The lady grabbed the picture, looked down, looked up, and looked back down again before moving the photo to the side.

"Jim here will be reading off with you." The lady pointed to an overweight man sitting more towards the side of the tables than behind it. "Whenever you're ready."

I cleared my throat and gave the go-ahead.

I tried my best to recite the lines, but it felt like there was a sudden roadblock in my brain, making it impossible to deliver a sneeze, let alone a scripted reply. And, to top it off, my legs could not stop trembling. Which meant now, on top of working through my sudden brain freeze-up, I had to keep my feet from involuntarily tap dancing. All while delivering the lines with my best sarcastic-airhead-ditz-bitch demeanor.

The plus side? If they needed a tall, stuttering model to imitate how humans react in small tremors, I was their girl.

"Hmm, okay," the lady said after I finished my part. "Can we do over pages three through eight, and maybe this time be a bit more…realistic? Alexis is a mean girl. She always gets her way. Show me that ferociousness."

I gave the lady my weakest, most-un-ferocious smile, took a breath, flipped to page three, and began again, trembling legs and all. This time around, instead of feeling like my brain had locked up, I felt like I had completely blacked out; like my consciousness had taken a backseat while some other, hopefully more confident, side of myself grabbed hold of the reigns.

From the looks on the people behind the table after I had finished my lines, that part of me must not have been that confident after all. That, or I had actually blacked out, and they had just witnessed me coming out of a slight coma. The silence filled every space of the austere receptacle they were calling a room. I stood there, genuinely wondering if I had fainted while on the job (again).

"Hmm, okay," the lady said again after a moment. "Thank you for your time. We'll be doing callbacks in about a week, so, if we like you, you'll be hearing from us soon."

"Oh, okay, thanks." I awkwardly held up the pages of the script until they were almost touching the side of my face. "Uh, do you want the, uh, script?"

"That? Just give it to Billy on the way out. Thanks again."

I turned and pushed opened one of the double doors. I walked back into the waiting area with an incredible uncertainty, as if I had wandered through a time warp and it was actually hours later instead of five minutes. I handed the script to the guy with the binder, who I assumed to be Billy, and I made my way back down the corridor and over to the elevator. I watched the lights at the top of the elevator as they slowly lit up the numbers for floor two, then floor three, then floor four, until the doors opened before me.

I made my way back home completely unsure of anything. What was I doing there in the first place? Did I really think I would get that role? Did I really think I'd walk away from that feeling even remotely good about myself? I was filled with nothing but a mix of nerves and disappointment. My self-esteem had been left behind alongside my 8 x 6 in that casting office.

As a surprise to no one, I never heard back from the casting people. I never heard anything more about the movie in general. But, even with such a disastrous first audition, I went on a few more after that. It was mostly for very small stuff, all of which I never got. But, somewhere in the midst of all those auditions, I found my nerve and stopped sucking so badly. I still made a fool out of myself, but it seemed to be a little less so each time.

As embarrassing as it was to shake like porcelain figurine on a runaway train, I'm still glad I did it. I went in as naïve as anyone could possibly be. I made an absolute fool of myself. Save for puking or fainting (or puking while fainting), the audition could not have gone any worse than it did. But life is too short not to make a fool out of yourself from time to time. And sometimes you need to make an ass out of yourself, just to see what you are capable of doing next. Life isn't just about pushing your limits and seeing what you're made of in the face of adversity. Sometimes it's about getting embarrassed and feeling humiliated and seeing where you can go from there.

Besides, deep down I know my big break will come when Models in Minor Earthquakes starts their casting process.

12

Model for a Day

The nicest thing about agency representation over freelancing is that the agency does all the negotiating for you. By the time you hear about the gig, you already know the day, the time, and, most importantly, the pay. When you are freelancing, that is entirely on you. And I learned the hard way that assuming you already know what the payment is—if there is going to be payment at all—is going to lead you down a nasty little road.

Once upon a time, I found a casting call looking for models to pose in wedding gowns for yet another wedding expo. I was just coming off my time as a pseudo-child bride and was more than happy to take whatever freelance wedding jobs came my way. I responded to the casting call, got the job, and got ready for one more modeling gig.

I did all the usual things a model does when it comes to working a show: I came in for a fitting, and then came in a second time for rehearsal (which will always make me laugh: yes, I need to rehearse walking in a straight line. I have never done this before. Please, teach me your ways). I talked with the owners about when and where I needed to be. I was so wrapped up in preparation for the show (as well as being literally wrapped up in tulle and sequins) that I never once thought about discussing compensation. I was used to my agency already having that unsavory little conversation about money, leaving me to put on my best model smile and sell those dresses for all they're worth (or at least for what the MSRP is). But, as the show date grew nearer, I couldn't stop that nagging feeling that I needed to discuss money. So I swallowed my ego and emailed the owner of the store about compensation.

When a show opts to not pay their models, they will usually find some excuse, such as, "This is for exposure!" or "Think of the great pictures you'll get!" forgetting the part where most attendants have absolutely no connections to the modeling world and a snapshot of a model walking down a makeshift runway in poor lighting isn't exactly going to help any model anywhere. So, when I read the first line of the response back ("Thank you for your question, Abby, but we are not going to be compensating our models with money for this show..."), I expected to read a nice little spiel about exposure or pictures. Instead, I got:

"What we are offering those who work with us next week is a chance to be a model for a day. So many girls wish they could do what models do, and this is their chance to feel like they can. Some of these girls might even grow up and become models themselves. I hope you understand."

It took a lot of effort to not to respond back, tell the boutique owner to buzz off, and immediately run in the opposite direction. I wanted to—oh, how I desperately wanted to—but I realized that I was the one who had dug this hole for myself. After all, it was my fault that I had waited until just before the show to discuss compensation. Had I asked at the beginning, I could've saved myself a world of trouble. So I ignored that sinking feeling in my gut and prepared for a show that I would be doing for absolutely free.

The expo wasn't a complete wash. I did get a chance to sample some of the free food from the vendors and I surreptitiously took pictures of myself in full makeup and hair. I strutted onto the tiny runway two or three times to clichéd dance music, linking arms with a teenaged boy (or a gay man who was easily twice my age), and smiled for all the would-be brides.

I quickly realized that I was a veteran in a sea of post-pubescent girls, most of whom were from the local high school. They giggled about getting their hair and makeup professionally done. One remarked that she wanted the same look for her senior prom. A couple others sheepishly admitted that they never thought that they would ever model. I smiled and nodded like a vapid trophy wife, never really contributing to the conversation but taking up space anyway.

For them, I could see the draw of being a model for a day. They were getting dolled up and put on display, something that doesn't really happen in their day-to-day lives. They had no idea how frustrating being an actual model can be, from hunting down go-sees to dealing with unhappy clients to nagging about payment. They never had anyone measure their waists and click their tongues and tell them that they're a whole half-inch bigger than what they had wanted. For them, it was still a world where photographers shout out, "Perfect! Sexy! Fantastic!" and models don't get out of bed for anything under $10,000. They were getting paid in living out all the fun parts of modeling, without any of the headaches.

And one of those headaches includes constant and open communication. It includes talking about the uncomfortable subject of money, even when part of you is shocked that anyone would pay you for anything. So, in a way, I got to pretend to be one of those models for a day as well, never worrying about the pragmatic aspects of modeling and instead pretending that getting my hair tugged and teased was "pampering" and that the would-be brides were actually paying attention to me and not the gown I was trying to sell.

I checked online afterwards in hopes of finding a few pictures of the show, at least to soften the blow of spending so much time (and gas money) on a gig that left me with nothing but memories. No such luck. I guess there is no photographic evidence of the time I was a model for a day.

13

The Big Reveal

There are some people who get into modeling purely for the attention.

I don't mean the attention of the photographers, makeup artists, and wardrobe stylists. I mean the attention they get when they reveal to their families and friends (and anyone who visits their social networking sites) that they model. They are quick to post modeling as a job and even quicker to talk about life as a model, even if they have never set foot into a photography studio in their entire lives. They just want people to look at the title "model" and marvel at how beautiful they must be to have such a job. Surely, their looks are now validated because they model. And everyone always told them that they should model, so why not just say they are?

And then there are some people who are more clever and covert in their ways to gain attention through their modeling.

I met one such girl a few years back. We did a few shows together and, as is the usual protocol for meeting people in the twenty-first century, we became friends through said various social networking sites.

At first, you couldn't immediately tell through her profiles that she was a model. She had her agency listed as a place of employment, but did not specify what her role was at said agency. There was a modeling photo here and there, but that was it. No gratuitous updates on the fact that she was a model. No deluge of pictures posted from one particular shoot. Just her and her life, all on display on her profile.

Then, somewhere along the line, she started getting cryptic.

"Life is tough when you have a secret," she posted one day. And, as is also part of the protocol for interaction in the twenty-first century, her cryptic message was met with an inundation of comments, all asking what was the matter. She kept mute about it—until the next day, when she posted:

"I have something I need to tell people, but I don't know how."

Again, people were falling over themselves, wondering what the big secret was. She continued this pattern, talking about being uncomfortable with such a "big reveal" and wondering out loud if she was ready for the world to know. Then, one bright, sunny day in June, this model wrote a long-winded paragraph about being true to who you are and not letting people get you down. She concluded the diatribe with:

"So, here it goes. Ladies and gentleman: I…model."

Sometimes life needs to come equipped with its own whomp-whomp sound effect.

From there, it was nothing but a steady stream of public declarations, talking about the horrible stigma that comes with modeling. People were buying into it left and right, telling her how wonderful it was that she was a model and to not let the naysayers get her down. You would've thought she was revealing the truth about her sexuality with the way people were supporting her and telling her to be true to who she is. I rolled my eyes and continued on with my internet life, thinking that was the end of it.

I was sorely mistaken.

For days and weeks later, all those social networking websites were flooded with pictures of her as a model, as well as an insistence that people ask her questions about the fashion industry so she could post a "Question and Answer" blurb on her various profiles. And like that, her online life became as much of an advertisement for her modeling as the girls who would write "I work as a MODEL for MODELING OMG!!" in their employment sections on their profiles.

At first, I was irked. It genuinely bothered me that she had drummed up all of those dramatics to garner attention to the fact that she was a model. Was it better or was it worse than those who, from day one, slammed it over the heads of anyone who would listen, shouting from the rooftops that they sometimes modeled?

But the more I thought about it, the more I realized that, really, I was no better than either of these types, allowing myself to get so worked up over another model's ruse for attention. Why would I care, if not for the fact that she gets all this attention, but I don't get the same recognition for not bringing it to everyone's attention? Maybe there was a bit of jealousy over the fact that her little portion of the internet world stopped for a moment to voice their support of her career.

And maybe I was jealous of her ingenuity. She did what advertising execs lose sleep trying to do: she garnered interest and curiosity over something that wouldn't usually garner such interest and curiosity. Through all her cryptic messages and through her "big reveal," she got more people to comment than if she had just said, "Yeah, I'm a model. Come and talk about me and praise my accomplishments."

In the beginning, I thought I was above the models who would lose their minds trying to get attention for their modeling. But all it took was one model with a game plan that would make her CEO at any firm to remind me that we're all looking for a bit of recognition, even if it's the unconscious and hypocritical need for attention over the fact that we're not publicly seeking out attention.

14

I'm Just Here for the Free Scrutiny

"Hi, it's nice to meet you. You pluck your eyebrows too much. Can you grow them out?"

All it takes is one unhappy client (or even potential client) to realize that a professional model's life does not entail absurd pampering and unearned praise. Sometimes all it takes is the icy stare of a designer during a go-see to realize that, more often than not, you will be picked apart and criticized (and then directed into uncomfortable poses in poorly-heated studios).

The hardest part about getting hired was always dealing with people who didn't have time for the model to feel okay. They had a pair of jeans, a juicer, or a nannying service to sell, and they weren't going to waste time sugarcoating the fact that the model looked like hell at a certain angle. You quickly realize that models don't make the big money because they're particularly pretty or skinny (or because they can smize); models make the big money because they can get yelled at for having awkward knees and still smile like that coffee maker makes the best damn coffee they have ever had. Models can be placed in the Atlantic Ocean in April in a bikini and act like they're loving their new bathing suit or Nantucket vacation, all the while processing the heckles from the creative director.

"Hey—can you stop shivering? It's blurring up the picture."

Modeling requires a thick skin, and I didn't realize how thick until I got signed to an agency. I would go to go-sees, hand over my comp card (which, for the folks at home, is simply a glorified index card with my pictures and my measurements), and watch as the casting director's face contorted into a snarl as she realized just how "fleshy" I was.

I once went to a casting call for a local runway show. I arrived wearing exactly what they had wanted the potential models to wear, did my walk, turned and twirled, and walked back. Usually, that would be the entire gist of the go-see for that individual model: hand in your comp card, smile (or smize), do the walk, smile/smize some more, walk back, go home. However, at the end of my walk, I was called to the front of the room again.

"Do you run?" the casting director said before I could even stop my forward momentum.

"Excuse me?"

"Running. Do you do it?"

"Um, yeah, I run," I answered, involuntarily cocking an eyebrow.

I also walk and climb and chew food and breathe. The whole scope of basic human experiences happens right here in this model's body!

"I could tell," said the director. "You have runner's legs."

I looked down at my legs—which were currently suffocating in the tightest "skinny jeans" that I had in my closet—and smiled.

"Um, thank you."

"That wasn't a compliment."

"Oh."

"You can go now," said the director with a self-satisfied smile. I responded with a halfhearted grin and returned back down the makeshift runway, feeling as much like a fashion model as a puppy dog in clogs.

I sat on the bench just outside the casting room, slipping off my high heels with a morose slowness. I returned my heels to my bag, put on my more sensible flats, and looked down at my legs. Even in the denim version of Spanx, my legs looked wide and muscular and obviously not meant for runway. I thought about my big thighs, my wide calves, and felt so painfully unattractive, like all that made me desirable rested in how spindly I could make my legs.

The door to the main hallway opened. A young girl with an impossibly narrow torso (and even more impossibly narrow legs) walked in and sat next to me.

"Are you here for the runway show?" she asked.

No, I'm just here for the free scrutiny.

"Yeah," I answered, my eyes still on my legs. "The sign-up is inside."

"Oh, good, thank you!" she answered, already standing up, hugging her portfolio to her chest.

"No problem," I replied. "Good luck."

The girl grinned so broadly that her eyes squinted. She sashayed her tiny hips, her little legs effortlessly moving down the hallway in her high heels, opened the door, and disappeared. I took one last look at my own legs before disappearing as well; only I was going in the opposite direction, as far as I could from the go-see and into the streets of Boston.

I had no interest in returning straight home. As was my usual MO when something was bothering me, I wandered around the Boston neighborhoods instead. I meandered up Newbury and down Boylston, from Copley to Back Bay to the South End and eventually into the Downtown area. I looped around Beacon Hill and walked the paths in the Esplanade before finding myself at the beginning of Newbury Street again. I wandered over to Kenmore Square, just taking in the sights and sounds and wondering where else I should go.

I thought about how long I had been walking, and how, even after I looped around the majority of Boston proper, I wasn't yet tired. Maybe some people can have the muscle stamina to walk for hours on end and still have very tiny legs, but I knew I wasn't one of them. I could keep walking because I had those thick running legs. The same reason I could run for an hour or survive an intense fitness class. And yes, it wasn't going to do me any favors in the modeling world, but the go-sees took up such a small amount of my everyday life. Would I ever really want to sacrifice all the time and energy that I spent seeing what I was physically capable of, all in an effort to have as little muscle mass a possible, so maybe—just maybe—I could walk up and down a catwalk for a designer who may or may not even care for me as a person?

And, like that, I felt a weight being lifted off my chest. A weight that, ironically enough, I couldn't have been able to hold on my own had I had tiny, underdeveloped muscles in my legs (and arms). I continued my walk until I felt a little more settled and caught the nearest T back home.

I never had a casting director (or any type of director) get on me for my "runner's legs" again, even after I started upping the mileage on my runs (making my legs just that much wider and that more muscular). But I was ready for it. I was ready to defend my runner's legs, my yogi's shoulders, my lifting-stuff-person's biceps. I was ready to counter all that free scrutiny with a speech about self-esteem. And I would've walked out of those casting rooms with absolutely no job or paycheck, but my head held high.

15

Some Actual, Serious Advice For Those Getting Into the Modeling World

All right, here we go. Some actual, serious advice. Let's see how far I can make it without adding in some snark.

Piece of Serious Advice #1: Be Honest With Yourself

The modeling world has the same rigorous standards when it comes to a certain "look" as MIT does when it comes to academic excellence. You wouldn't apply to MIT with a 2.1 GPA in hopes that you'll be that special student who turns the entire academic world on its ear. If you're 5'2" and have hopes of making it big as a mainstream fashion model, I apologize in advance. Maybe you'll find photographers who enjoy working with you. Maybe you'll find a local club or store that is hosting a community fashion show and wants you to walk. Maybe you'll even carve out a nice little niche as a freelancer. But, most likely, you'll be Sisyphus, tirelessly pushing a boulder up a hill, only to watch it roll all the way back down.

And that's just an extreme example. There are models whose

dreams of walking the high fashion catwalks are dashed because their faces are "too commercial." There are models who get passed over because they have absurdly large eyes and the current trend is absurdly large lips. There are models who go from a size 0 to a size 2 and stop hearing the phone ring.

I would never go so far as to tell someone, "Stop before you start," but be realistic. Do your homework. Want to be a fashion model? Find out what the current industry-standard measurements are. Maybe you'll eke by with your current look. Maybe you won't.

And, for the love of God, stop pointing to Kate Moss as an example of short girls being able to model high fashion. She is 5'7" and with a face that (at least in the 80s and 90s) stopped people in their tracks. She had enough "it" factor to help usher in heroin chic at a time when supermodels were comparatively "fleshy"-looking. If you think you're powerful enough to usher in a completely new genre of modeling, then go right ahead. Prove me wrong.

Piece of Serious Advice #2: Not All Agencies Are Created Equal

…If that has not been made abundantly clear by the end of this collection of essays (anyone interested in signing up for the Haha We Took Your Child's Money Agency?). Do your research when it comes to agencies. Even "legit" agencies can sometimes swindle their models. In the New England area alone, I've watched three separate agencies bottom out, go bankrupt, and pack up and leave—usually without paying models for jobs that they had done months and months prior.

Talk with models in the area about local agencies. You'll notice a pattern after a while. Agencies that have been in the business for decades are usually a good sign, but it's not always a guarantee.

A proper agency will not try to pawn off "classes" on you. They will not charge you a "website profile" fee. They will not shove a list of photographers in front of you and say that you must work with these photographers (for an astronomical fee) before you are "ready" for real work. They might charge you the cost of printing for your comp cards. But that should be about it.

The more an agency charges you for various things, the less confident they are that they will make their money through finding you work. And you're with the agency so they can find you work, not so they can charge you money to have your face on their website.

On top of being honest with yourself about modeling, be honest with yourself about agencies. Do you really need an agency? Are you the type of fashion or commercial model who would benefit from the help of an agency? Do you live in an area that has a decent fashion or commercial market (for example: New York City versus Thar-Be-Dragonville, Wyoming)? Or do you just want to say that you're an agency-represented model? A lot of shady agencies prey on boys and girls who just want to say they're agency-repped. Be smart, be alert, and be willing to walk away from a bum deal.

And if you get that elusive interview with an agency, don't be afraid to ask them questions as well. What is the frequency of go-sees for a model with your look? What is the general protocol if a model is in need of a better portfolio? Does the agency charge printing fees, or website fees? Remember: you are there to make them money in return for them finding you jobs. This is a two-way street. Don't feel like you have to acquiesce and go into the interview begging at their feet.

Piece of Serious Advice #3: Avoid Those Stupid Modeling Schools

I'm honestly shocked that, in this day and age, I have to give this advice. I won't name the names of certain modeling schools, but they're all moneymaking scams. In all fairness, some of these models will go on to have great careers. But they were going to, anyway. They had the right look. They were willing to log in the hours. The fact that they went to "modeling school" does not really factor in to the equation.

Modeling school is for girls who would like to pretend to be a model and are willing to spend a ludicrous amount of money to do so. Most people in the fashion world will tell you that modeling schools actually do more harm than good, as they teach girls trite, clichéd ways of posing and give the girls an unrealistic view on how the modeling world works.

So, seriously and honestly, save your money. If you have the right look (and are the right age), all you need are a few snapshots to send to agencies.

And speaking of: if you are sending snapshots to an agency, make sure they are shots of you with minimal makeup, hair pulled back (if you have long hair), in a simple outfit, and with a white background behind you. And you only need three: headshot, full body shot, and profile. Keep the selfies and the pictures of you at the club (or dressed up as Sexy Ninja Turtle for Halloween) at home.

Piece of Serious Advice #4: Prepare to Get Rejected

Rejection is the name of the game. We all know it by now. But there's still a part of us that holds on to the idea that, somehow, we'll be different. We'll be the one that people fall over themselves to book. We'll be the one that never gets rejected. Even when we start getting rejected left and right, even as we talk more and more about how often one gets rejected, we still hold out that hope.

But that's just how it is. It's a subjective, picky industry. They'll pass you over because you didn't do your makeup the way that they would've done your makeup for the job. They'll pass you over because they wanted a blonde with green eyes and you're a blonde with hazel eyes. They'll pass you over because the previous model was a pill during her go-see and their annoyance lingered as you came in.

In an industry saturated with would-be models, rejection is more common now than ever before. Understand that, and understand that understanding that won't make the rejection any easier.

Piece of Serious Advice #5: Don't Let the Bastards Get You Down

I've been told I would be better off marketing myself as a plus-size model because I had no business in the "standard-size" industry. I've been told that I was too big, too small, too American, too sexy, too girl-next-door. I've had photographers and coordinators talk to me like I'm a preschooler who can't color within the lines. I've seen pictures of me get so edited and distorted that I couldn't recognize the girl in front of me. I've had people talk about my failings as a model with me still in the room, and loud enough so that I knew that they weren't trying to hide their disdain.

I cannot stress enough: this is a tough, tough, tough, tough, tough industry. There is always someone slimmer than you, more "fresh-faced" than you, and better able to walk in 5" heels than you can. You cannot let it get you down. If you start internalizing the beatings the modeling world can give you, you will not last long.

…And in case you fell asleep during my first essay: don't tell people that, "everyone said you should model." You sound delusional. Or smug. Or smugly delusional.

<u>16</u>

Things I Have Learned from the Modeling World (That Are Actually Viable in the Real World)

Lesson #1: Expectation is Not Reality

I've long lost count of the number of shoots where I expected things to go one way, only to watch them go another. Or the number of times I found that the final image came out in a completely different way than what I was anticipating. I went into freelance work—as well as agency representation—expecting things to go a lot differently than they did. I learned that there are a lot of "boring" modeling jobs: pictures for internal purposes only, fit modeling (where you try on samples and stand really still while they figure out how to modify the outfit), modeling for meetings at retail headquarters, and so on, and so forth. I learned just how unglamorous and monotonous modeling can actually be. I learned that a go-see for even the biggest names can still be just you walking around in uncomfortable heels in the back of a warehouse or in a nondescript office building.

Reality is never what you imagined it would be. Sometimes it's better. Sometimes it's worse. And sometimes it's just different. It's not worth wasting time and energy trying to predict how things are going to turn out. Just go with the flow and keep your eyes and ears pealed.

Lesson #2: Stop Being Scared and Stick Your Neck Out

I remember when I finally gave into the idea of modeling. I had just finished my very first job for my friend's band, doing weird quasi-artistic shots for the CD covers of their demo songs. Artistic shots, like poking at a running shower head while fully clothed and outside the bathtub, or pretending I was staring at a green orb on the ground. But that's for another time.

I finished up these shoots realizing that I really, really liked modeling. I made a profile on a modeling website and sat back, wondering when the hordes of photographers and clothing companies would be banging down my door in an effort to work with me.

Spoiler alert: it didn't happen.

As a freelancer, it took searching out casting calls and contacting the people I needed to contact and networking as best as I could. It took sticking my neck out and getting rejected and doing it all over again.

When I finally worked up the courage to go agency hunting, I sent out my pictures, even though the very thought of getting rejected on an agency level scared the piss out of me. And I did get rejected. But I also got signed by one of these agencies. And when the time came for me to venture out into the modeling world again at the ripe age of 26, I sent out my pictures to the top Boston agency—an agency that had passed on me many years ago—fully recognizing that I might get rejected yet again.

And I almost did. Somehow, dumb luck (which I will get into in a moment) prevailed and the director decided to ask for a few snapshots before potentially telling me to buzz off. He liked what he saw and called me in for a meeting. I was signed that day (with the understanding that my portfolio was steering me in absolutely the wrong direction—another thing I'll get to in a moment).

The likelihood that success is going to fall into your lap is slim to none. Very rarely does someone get "discovered" while walking their dog or pumping their gas. They usually get "discovered" by working hard, taking chances, and getting over the fear of rejection.

It's the same with anything in life. You need to stop worrying about the negatives, take a risk, and stick your neck out.

Lesson #3: Sometimes Dumb Luck Will Win Out

Throughout the years, I've met a lot of striking, talented models. The types of models who can walk into a room and immediately attract everyone's attention. The types of models whose faces were completely unforgettable. The types of models that any client should rightfully lose their mind to have. These models could sell a product, a service, a fashion line, or an editorial idea without any effort.

And I've seen those models go absolutely nowhere with their careers.

I remember getting a job for a commercial purely because I had showed up with a pearl necklace on and they had imagined their commercial queen wearing a similar necklace. I remember losing a job because the person in front of me knew the client and was busy talking to said client when I came in. People have snagged jobs because they were the first, the last, the perfectly-in-the-middle person to show up to the go-see. People have lost jobs because they had sneezed in the middle of the line reading and had to start all over again.

Hard work, determination, and talent are key for any successful venture. But sometimes you need that fourth ingredient: dumb luck. Luck can never replace hard work and talent, but sometimes it can win out over both.

Lesson #4: Learn to Sell Yourself

As I mentioned before, I was nearly rejected a second time from my now-agency because I sent in the wrong pictures. To this day, I thank my lucky stars that the director was feeling benevolent and asked for a few snapshots to get a better idea of what I looked like.

In our meeting, he told me point blank that I was a commercial model who hadn't been selling herself properly. There was nothing in my portfolio that would make J.Crew or Macy's go, "This girl will help sell our khaki pants!" I held my breath, waiting for the director to hand me the list of photographers that I must work with (for an astronomical fee) before I could actually work-work. That thankfully never happened. Instead, I got signed and was put on the list for trade (aka free) shoots to bring my portfolio back on the right track.

Maybe it's the low self-esteem talking, but I have never been comfortable with the idea of selling myself. Brand management, image management, management management…it's just not me. But sometimes you have to do it, especially if it means the difference between getting ahead and getting nowhere. Have the confidence to showcase your strengths and be unapologetic when you refuse to be pigeonholed.

Lesson #5: Some People Just Cannot Be Pleased

If you haven't already by this point in the book, recognize that there is no truth in the shows that make photo shoots out to be this flattery-fest, where the photographer gently guides the model into whatever pose variation he is looking for, followed by, "Yes! That is great! Perfect! You are perfect!" I have yet to do a proper, paying job where I was inundated by praise. Usually, I was just poked and prodded and moved about until I was in the exact pose they were looking for. And they were not afraid to tell me when I was doing something that they felt wouldn't properly sell their product, even for a single frame.

Some of these clients would balance this out with gentle praise when I was doing what they wanted (not exactly to the levels of "Yes! Perfect!" but, hey, something is better than nothing). Most wouldn't. Most would stand idly back and only speak when I was doing something wrong.

And I always seemed to be doing something wrong. My hands were too stiff (or too limp), or I was walking at a wrong angle away from the center point. It didn't matter if the end product came out great, or if the things they swore I was doing wrong was actually solving a problem with the shoot. I was simply a bag of meat who was inadequately selling their product.

The only thing I could do was tolerate it until it was time to clock out. I couldn't take it personally. They had a product or a service to sell and I was little more than a prop in their promotion scheme. I wasn't going to make them happy, and it wasn't until I realized that it wasn't my job to make them happy in the first place did I stop letting them bother me. Some people are impossible to please, and all I can do get the job done and go on with my life.

Lesson #6: No One Is Going to Do It For You

I remember when I landed my first agency. I emailed a few of the photographers that I knew, telling them the good news. A few replied with, "That's awesome!" One insightful photographer replied with, "Congratulations – now the real work begins."

Having an agency can be super useful in terms of finding

clients. The bigger and more reputable the agency, the more likely people will come to them hoping to hire their models. But, as I've learned, that doesn't mean that they'll create work for you. At the end of the day, I'm still the one going on go-sees, attempting to amaze the clients, hoping to land the job.

And if I land the job? It's on me not only to show up on time, prepared in the exact way that is expected of me (as well as prepared in ways that they hadn't previously mentioned, as people always seem to forget something and, for some reason, people tend to look at the model to solve it). And once the job is done, it's my duty to fill out the necessary paperwork—to get the client to fill out the necessary paperwork—and to file it in a timely fashion. If I mess up, it makes not only me look bad, but the agency as well. I can't sit back and expect others to do the work for me.

It's the same with the rest of my life: if I want something accomplished, I need to go out and do it myself. I can't sit back and expect others to fulfill my dreams or accomplish my goals. The only one who can do it is myself.

Lesson #7: For the Love of God, Get the Idea of Fame Out of Your Head

Like a proper millennial, the concept of becoming famous is always there, lurking behind all the rational goals and dreams. "I hope to find a fulfilling career." "I hope I can get my work published." "I hope to get bloody famous and be adored by millions of complete strangers for practically no reason." I remember being a kid, looking around at all these adults with their sensible jobs in their suburban homes, and wondering, "Why the hell aren't all these people tripping over themselves to become famous instead?"

Well, because fame is not only an irrational goal, but an unsustainable one to boot. We'd collapse as a country if we all gave up our jobs and tried to get on TV.

And for what? So people can look at us for a little bit? Give us attention? Criticize our every move and watch as our (literal or metaphorical) slip-ups turn into GIFs and news fodder? And that's not getting into the fact that fame is fickle, short-lived, and has proven disastrous for even the strongest spirits.

The first thing I learned when I got into modeling was that the majority of the work out there wasn't as the girl who poses for Vogue, but as the girl who is a bit too happy to be using that brand new toaster. Or as part of a romantic couple who is non-threateningly into each other as they sit by a brand new car. The vast majority of work is through channels like catalogues and packaging pictures and maybe the occasional advertisement. And yes, you technically get your picture out there—but who really sees it? Who sees you when they're buying laundry detergent with your smiling mug on the back? Who will ever stop you at a store and say, "Aren't you that woman in that Talbot's catalogue?" What paparazzo is going to care about the model who posed for a fledgling bathrobe company?

It scares me sometimes to think about the obsession with fame, especially since the second half of Generation Y (and the kids after that generation) are even more about it than I (or my peers) ever were. Don't believe me? Just look at the shows available now for tweens. Throw a stone and you'll most likely hit a TV show where the main character is a rock star or a movie star or a band hoping to "make it big."

Actually, if you throw a stone, you'll most likely just hit your TV and potentially damage it. So ixnay on the owingthray.

The world is full of people just hoping to make a living, while a select handful of other people walk red carpets and go on interviews and get their pictures surreptitiously taken while leaving a coffee shop. And while there is nothing wrong with acting or singing (or modeling), one just has to approach it understanding that, most likely, it'll be simply another job without all the fame and glory.

Lesson #8: You're Exactly What Someone is Looking for, Somewhere

The hardest part about modeling was getting passed over time and time and time again. My bust was too big for the samples. My look was too commercial. I had brown hair and they were looking for "raven." I would give my all at go-sees and casting calls and watch as girls who (and I might be naïve and biased here) had absolutely nothing on me get the gigs instead.

And then every once in a while I would not only get a gig, but get sought out specifically to be hired for the job. I had the exact measurements they were looking for. I had exactly the "maternal smile" they were hoping to find. I was just the right amount of athletic. They took one look and God help the rest of the models.

I learned that, while rejection is the name of the game, I'm always going to be exactly what someone is looking for, eventually. Whether it is looks or personality, be it in the professional world or the dating world, what others have over me is irrelevant, because there's always someone out there looking for an exact type of someone—a someone that I can completely fulfill. I'm not going to be everyone's ideal, so focusing on the times I get passed over – be it the modeling industry or in real life—is a colossal waste of time.

Lesson #9: The World is Callous and Shallow; It's Your Job to Not Become That Way, As Well

Coming as a surprise to no one, mainstream modeling is a pretty superficial profession. No one cares about how good of a person you are, or how creative you can be. Do you have the look they are going for? No? Get out.

And even if you get the job, there's no guarantee they'll be kind and understanding as you figure out what they want from you (see: "Some People Just Cannot Be Pleased"). It's your job to do what they ask without snapping back. It's your job to go to the go-sees with a smile on your face, even if they're scowling at you.

You'll meet models at casting calls and go-sees who would

probably think nothing of pushing you down the stairs if it meant they got the gig instead of you. There's a chance you might even deal with people at your own agency who have no issues treating you like a piece of meat—a piece of meat that is never living up to the expectations they set out for you when they signed you.

The modeling world—and the world at large—is a pretty cruel place. It's up to you to decide whether or not that turns you into a cruel person as well. Are you going to be mean and selfish because some of the people around you are, or are you going to overcome that and walk away a decent human being? The world gives you every reason in the book to become callous. It's your job not to become that way as well.

Epilogue

I really have nothing to say here. I just felt that I needed some way to close out this book.

So, yeah. Modeling.

Hey, look over there!

About the Author

Abby Rosmarin is a writer, a martial art instructor (tai chi counts, people), and a model. She's a hardcore Bostonian (even though she moved up to New Hampshire three years ago) and a proud owner of an English degree (which, as the years progress, has proven to be little more than a really expensive wall decoration). Her favorite pastimes include busting a dance move when doing housework, having philosophical arguments with herself while driving, and refusing to admit that ska is dead. She currently lives with her husband in a small town in the mountains alongside her two cats, her guinea pig, and a whole coop of chickens (and by "whole coop," she means three). Don't forget to follow her on Twitter @thatabbyrose.